THE
SELF-
COMPASSION
PROJECT

How to become **emotionally stronger,**
more effective, and **happier**
by giving yourself a break

RITA DESNOYERS-GARCIA

Printed in the United States of America

First Printing, 2019

ISBN 978-0-9824376-2-9

Edited by Amy McGlinn
www.amymcglinn.com

Book Design by Heather Kern
www.popshopstudio.com

Cover Photograph by Fnadya76
www.istockphoto.com

To find out more about Rita Desnoyers-Garcia and her work,
visit www.BecomingAwake.com

Is this book right for you?

I'll cut to the chase: if you're a woman who is always striving for more, has been locked up in the self-help section of the bookstore and is hoping for enlightenment to strike while still struggling with some stubborn issues, you may have overlooked something.

That stone that perhaps went unturned?

Self-compassion.

I noticed this void in myself and my clients over the years. Everyone was eager for improvement and change, but we all were blind to being a little kinder to ourselves.

We're under the spell of "if it ain't working, work harder!" It's a part of our culture. I don't know about you, but I was never told to be kind and gentle with myself - nor even to laugh at my own human foibles! I was told to buckle down and keep going. Keep a stiff upper lip. Keep calm and carry on.

What self-compassion can do for you

If we can agree that self-compassion (and a sense of humor) may be an ingredient that is missing from your *Wonderful Life Recipe*, let's move on to why it makes sense to include it in cups more than pinches. If you're working harder and harder to "get it together" or "overcome some issues" and you're chasing your tail, you'll need a new strategy. The old one is predictably no longer serving you. Tapping into self-compassion is a little-known strategy, but a highly effective one.

Self-compassion creates space to look at things from another angle; it supports you to have the courage and fortitude to see something new and make changes. Self-compassion helps you accept what's going on and integrate parts of you that you've forgotten, repressed, and rejected so that you are no longer working against yourself. Self-compassion is the safety net so you can walk on the tightrope of change into the unknown.

Self-compassion is not about being soft and wussy, but being brave, strong, clear, and willing to laugh and create something new in your life. This is not woo-woo, airy-fairy stuff. It's foundational in creating and being in the new world that is coming into fruition right now.

Self-compassion allows for a new perspective of life because you are no longer a victim.. When you go through the exercises in this book, you realize that you are the heroine of your story and the co-creator of your life where things happen *for* you.

My quick self-compassion story

I decided to skip the long intro and say this about myself:

I got help with self-compassion by mistake. I reached out to a coach in desperation – I needed help with my floundering business. It looked less like a business and more like Lucy and Ethel trying to keep up with the chocolate assembly line by eating and stuffing the chocolates down their shirt! I thought he could help me "close" clients and then I'd be successful and happy. I was going to save myself and my family (oh, boy...). However, this coach was really coming in to put me on a different course.

Our first meeting, on the phone, was to see if we were a good match. I told him what was going on; about how I was trying to run a business, being a mother of three little ones, about my dream of retiring my husband and having a successful and happy life. And how what I was doing was not working (surprise!). If only I could learn to "close" clients, everything would be better.

His simple response: "Can you be gentle and kind to yourself right now?"

I was stunned. Wha?

That was an option? It's like I had never heard of this before. I immediately started to cry. I felt a sense of relief that I was being given permission to allow myself a little compassion. At the same time, my mind went into overdrive. How is being gentle and kind going to help me right now? Is this a con? Am I being punked?

Being gentle will not get me where I want to go. Is Oprah gentle with herself? I need answers (and tissues) now, not touchy-feely solutions. I felt confused by the relief and yet my mind wanted to talk me out of it.

The strength of self-compassion

At that point, I knew this coach was someone I needed to work with even as my mind was cautioning me.

He explained that we would be talking nuts and bolts strategies about this situation in my life but first, it was really important to take a moment of compassion for myself. We discussed my resistance and what my mind was telling me. It turns out, my mind was giving a lot of resistance (hint: you may feel resistance too when you go through these exercises). My mind was saying things like, "Don't feel pity for yourself, work harder."

We teased out how "having pity for yourself" is not the same as being kind and compassionate with yourself. Having pity implies that I'm in a lesser position, whereas compassion is about understanding, support, seeing more clearly, taking a step back and empowerment as an equal. Believe it or not, laughing at yourself also is good sign!

Working on my beliefs about myself and the world around me, I realized that compassion for myself was the gateway into understanding, clear decision-making, self-love, real change, and expansion.

Working smarter, not harder

Over time, I also realized more and more, that working harder didn't work well for me anymore. I saw how I could work with passion but use my energy more efficiently and effectively by coming from a place of deep compassion for myself. I wasn't working against myself and my limited beliefs, I was using the power of the Universe (Yes!) to guide me. I was allowing the Universe to do its job. I had read this in many books and heard about it in many videos, but never realized that self-compassion was the key to working with the Universe.

(Mind blown!)

I was tapping into something very powerful when I allowed myself the space to feel compassion for these parts of my psyche, where I was working on old programs of my past that no longer served me. And compassion was my way to understand, shift and revise these old programs into ones that are more integrated, powerful, and loving.

I was reprogramming my beliefs around what constitutes success and happiness. The process itself felt as good as the end goal.

I can almost guarantee self-compassion is what has been missing

I started to allow myself some self-compassion (thank Goddess.). I went through the steps that I describe in this book. It's a journey of honesty, humility, humor, shock, and love. It's not always comfortable but it's better than how miserable I was before.

I'm happier, kinder, more humble, patient, and open. Maybe funnier?

It's important to know that self-compassion is not only doable for you, but it's also essential if you want any change in your life. If you're like me, you've read, you've gone to the workshops and seminars to "improve" and "develop" yourself. Some of it worked and some of it didn't. Some you may still do now and some you stopped a long time ago (no judgment). None of it really works well if you don't have compassion for yourself along the way.

Self-compassion says, "I'm open and listening... I'm holding space for me." That new compassionate relationship changes how you deal with EVERYTHING. **It's a game changer.** When you have a little more self-compassion, you not only change, but the world also changes because you start to perceive it differently and be in it differently. With all the polarization in the world right now, one of the biggest steps you can make to "be the change" is to have compassion for yourself and others. It creates a new world where compassion is the default. You want a more compassionate Earth? Start with you. Start with self-compassion.

How this book works

This book has three sections: **Self-compassion**, **Acceptance**, and **Integration**. Each section has exercises, strategies, and techniques for you to read and do. They may challenge you. They may make you feel some discomfort. They may stretch you.

That is normal, by design, and good for you. Nothing new comes without thinking or doing something new. This is about creating new pathways in your brain so self-compassion is the new default for you. Like an exercise program, it may take you longer and be more challenging in the beginning, but once you get the hang of it, it will take less time and you'll see results that will encourage you to keep it going. I recommend you do the exercises **for 30 days** at least, so you really do get the hang of it.

Having said all that, take an attitude of curiosity, play, and experimentation with yourself. Try to not take yourself too seriously. Laughing at parts of you is key to healing. We are a balance of it all! You can't get this wrong. You've got nothing to lose and everything to gain by diving in and sticking with the exercises over **the next 30 days**. This book will keep you focused so you can collect your energy and go for it.

How to get started

Read through the next few pages including the complete self-compassion exercise steps.

Then go back, when you have at least 30 minutes (it may take less or more, and you can always revisit it) of uninterrupted, private time to complete the self-compassion exercises (*Calm the Storm, Switch it, The Game Changer*). Take time to let yourself write what comes up, use your imagination to picture your parts as they reveal themselves, ask questions and let yourself write – even if it doesn't make logical sense to you. If you're not a writer, **dance, sing, draw, paint** what comes up. It's all about **having what's inside you come out so you can observe it, let it go, understand it better than before.** All the exercises are about expanding your intuition, your creativity, your higher mind, and your heart.

When you've completed at least one round of the self-compassion exercises, read through *Acceptance* and then read *Integration*.

This workbook is designed for your own pace and practice. It's not something you read and then add to your collection of self-help books. It's here to use over and over again. It's here for drawing, writing, visualizing, and reading aloud. By the end of 30 days, it should look nice and worn – if not beaten up!

Let's go!

I'll walk you through everything in this workbook. I'm here whenever you need me (just read!). If you can have that "we're in this thing together" attitude (that's you and your Higher Self), or even imagine having a friend/mentor beside you (hello there!) as you venture forth, it will help a lot!

*"Love and compassion are necessities, not luxuries.
Without them, humanity cannot survive."*

—Dalai Lama XIV, <u>The Art of Happiness</u>

COMPASSION

Part 1

"Compassion is when the Divine abides with you."
—Rita Desnoyers-Garcia

What is compassion?

Compassion is one of those words that many people define differently. People also seem to define compassion in a way that can prevent them from being compassionate toward others or themselves. (Ironic, no?)

> Compassion is defined as:
>
> ## "com|pas|sion
>
> sympathetic consciousness of others' distress together with a desire to alleviate it." *(Merriam Webster)*

I define compassion as a *level of consciousness*. It's not sympathy- as in "I feel badly for you but I'm above you/too bad for you." It's more like, *" I see you in a whole way. I see what situation you've got going on. I see you have shadows and I see your light. I connect with you, as I too, have shadows and light. I am not above or below you. We each possess parts of each other."*

Compassion is a high vibration and doesn't lower itself to feel badly, but is about recognition of our common humanity and divinity. It is a high level of consciousness that doesn't judge or blame. It sees clearly, discerns, and takes on the ability to respond from that higher state of consciousness.

Compassion is the opposite of denial. It denies nothing and accepts everything. It doesn't allow for harm to self or others. Compassion creates the healthiest of boundaries while still keeping a connection to the higher self of the other person. I see compassion as the state of consciousness in which the Divine can conduct its business. When you feel compassion, you are feeling what the Universe feels for all its creation – the connection of the Divine to the Divine in you and within another.

Compassion is not always easy. It is not always light and effortless. In fact, it may feel difficult at times. We will work through that feeling together in this book.

Making compassion your default

The exercises in this book will show you – or remind you, really– that you can feel compassion for yourself and change your life. When you live your life from a place of self-compassion, you start to see everything through the eyes of the Divine. The question is, do you believe you have the capacity to hold a sympathetic consciousness for yourself in order to alleviate your own distress? It's an important question to ask. (Ask yourself, not your doctor, if self-compassion is right for you!)

Many times people want to change their situation but they readily think they are not capable of being the least bit kind, gentle, sympathetic, or compassionate for themselves. They might have been self-compassionate a long time ago before they were talked out of it. They were taught to be tough on themselves, to work harder and faster to make a change. Being kind and gentle was not a viable option. I know it was not on the table for me. The idea that being kind to myself was productive at all was almost laughable. A foolish idea for lazy people that led to denial, failure, and staying stuck. Ironically, I didn't notice that my "get tough" strategy was delivering the failure, denial, and stuckness that I feared.

Do you really want to alleviate your distress?

You might say, "Yes!" but ask it again. Most people don't really want to alleviate their distress. They want to keep it around like an old friend (an old annoying, crazy friend). They are "doing things." They are "real." Most people argue for their own misery. They fight for "unhappiness" because they believe that is what they deserve, need, or are destined to experience. Feeling happy or peaceful feels dangerous (I know you're nodding in agreement right now). And, they will sacrifice their peace and happiness as if it comes with a price – the price of change or discomfort or looking at themselves in a new way.

This seems counterintuitive, but hear me out. Most people are swimming in anxiety, depression, fear, anger, distress of some sort. At some point, the distress becomes toxic and we want to get rid of it. However, most people try to repress it with some sort of temporary stop-gap measure of numbing or distraction, and never get to the core issue that keeps the low-level distress there in the first place. The numbing/distraction strategy works temporarily, but the distress is still there on a "liveable" level until the next time. Drinking, eating, watching TV, going online, shopping or even compulsive exercising are some examples of numbing/distracting strategies. Sound familiar?

Take a quick look at what you may be doing in your daily life to distract from,

or numb the pain. You may want to make a list of things you do to escape the pain. It will help you identify when you are leaving your higher level of consciousness. (Hint: I left a big blank space for you to write in. Do not disappoint!)

Alleviating distress requires a different strategy. It's not about numbing or distraction. It's about going deeper and moving into the pain that's happening. It's about becoming present in what's happening, feeling it, asking questions, getting curious, releasing, taking new action as necessary, accepting, integrating. It takes a higher level of sympathetic consciousness to desire the alleviation of the distress at its root. It requires self-compassion.

Journal or draw here about which activities keep you numb or distracted

Making room for your new life

Many people need help with this process from a therapist, a healer, a health practitioner, a total stranger on a plane...is that just me? However, you can learn to use self-compassion on your own. If you are dedicated to alleviating your distress, you can do a whole lot all by yourself. And, you aren't really alone. You are allowing the Divine to flow through you and guide you. Yay! Divine!

How do I know? I've been where you are in the process and I've used self-compassion to heal a whole lot in me. I've used the opportunity to have self-compassion to alleviate distress, get clearer about who I am and what I want, know what action to take, and where to get help. I've used self-compassion to become a better parent, wife, friend, sister, human. I've used it to weather through some tough situations in my life and be able to accept some things that before completely broke me. I was able, with self-compassion, to pick up the broken pieces and put them back together in a new, stronger, more integral way. I've become happier, more welcoming with healthier boundaries, abundant, peaceful, passionate, clear, loving, patient, humble, open, firm and kind.

In short, self-compassion has changed who I am in the world and the world I live in. I wrote this book because I know it will do the same for you if you allow it to.

For any of the following strategies and exercises, you can use the journaling space provided. Those blank pages are for writing, drawing, doodling, coffee cup stains, ripping, whatever suits your fancy. Don't forget to have a sense of humor! Recording what you felt and how it shifted (if it did) gives you some objective information to see any progress and encourages you to keep going!

Strategy 1

Calm the storm

The mechanics of self-compassion are pretty simple. It starts with the breath. Going inward for a moment, taking a breath and letting it out, can be an act of self-compassion. It may not stop your mind from badgering you, but it will start a process of relaxation and you can release some tension. Compassion is about relaxing internally. When we breathe through the nose deeply and exhale gently through the mouth, we signal to the body to relax, slow down. When the body can relax, we are better able to observe our minds going all over the place in thought. When we can observe ourselves, we take on the perspective of the Compassionate Self. We separate a bit from the idea that we are our thoughts or that we are trapped in our situation. When we relax in our bodies through our breath, we are more likely to feel some compassion come through. Focused, relaxed breathing calms the storm of thoughts and emotions inside.

Take a moment to come to center. Sometimes, doing that is enough. Breathe in through the nose and out the mouth. Jot down how you feel afterward. You can use this whenever you need it during the day.

Journal here any thoughts, feelings, images that come up

SELF-COMPASSION

Strategy
2

Switch it

When breathing is not doing it for you, there are other things to do! Here's a process I use when I have a negative feeling:

Allow yourself to feel what you feel- name it, identify it; sadness, boredom, anger, etc. Then see the opposite of that; joy, excitement, calm, etc. Say to yourself, "May I bring more joy/excitement/calm into my life". You are calling in what you need to come back to balance. You don't feel any lack. You are calling your desired state forth from the Divine within. This is what self-compassion and acceptance does; it puts you in a state of the Divine so you can have room for something new.

Journal here any thoughts, feelings, or images that come up

The act of being self-compassionate allows the innate Divine to work through you. It is an invitation and activation of your Divinity. Do you have any part of you that has been mistreated, has taken on a burden from your ancestors, has been avoided, repressed, ignored, and is hungry for the Divine within you? The more this part lashes out in a misguided attempt to protect itself, the more it needs your Divine nature, in the form of self-compassion.

How to be strong, calm and brave

I've done a lot of "release" work - mucho! I've read all the books, watched the videos, released a bunch of stuff – and still do. Release work really does help. However, sometimes something more is required to get at that thing that doesn't seem to want to go. You need some emotional Drano! It needs you to address it head-on. It needs a "game changer", in a loving way. It needs to be heard and loved and accepted and recognized and integrated within you so that it stops hurting you and others.

I developed some steps for self-compassion - not by myself, but by reading, watching, doing, and learning from many teachers over years. These steps have helped me tremendously. I've used them in countless situations. I've taught them and witnessed people uncover parts of themselves that they never knew existed. Now, they could not only see parts of their psyche, but learn from those parts. They invite that awakened part to work with them and integrate.

Self-compassion is the balm that heals all wounds. It is a balm that is readily available within each of us at each moment. It is so powerful, so simple, so Divine. We don't use it because we did not learn how or why to use it. We were taught to be hard on ourselves, be tough with ourselves, to repress and gloss over our 'wounded' parts. Kindness and gentleness has not been a 'go-to' place.

The game changer

The following steps are here for when you need a little extra help or you are new to this kind of process. Keep in mind that a "part" may be feminine or masculine or both! I refer to a part as feminine, but don't let that box you in. (There is no box! Mind blown AGAIN).

1) Feel what you are feeling. You are feeling something as a result of perceiving your world. Your perceptions are based on your personal, familial, and societal history. We decide something feels "good" or "bad," "beautiful," "ugly," etc. We have thoughts-and we have feelings about those thoughts. One of the first things we tend to do when we feel anything (especially a negative feeling), is ignore, avoid, or rationalize. **When was the last time you felt what you felt? When have you taken a moment to feel into what's happening within you right now?** Maybe it feels frightening to really feel the anxiety or hatred or jealousy. Recognize and acknowledge that you are having a feeling experience. You may blame this feeling on the actions of another (and that may be very valid), but many times that deflects from feeling the emotion.

Take a moment, close your eyes and feel what you feel. Connect to your body. **Are there areas in your body where you feel tension, constriction, or pain?** Put your hand there, breathe into that area, and send it love and compassion.

Journal here about anything that comes up for you

2) Thank this part for showing itself! Sometimes, your feeling is an expression of a "part" of you that needs attention and is telling you something. Perhaps it has been there for years, to warn you and protect you. Maybe it got you through your childhood and was a survival mechanism. You may have been discouraged from listening to it. It's up for a reason; to be expressed, heard, and to serve you. It also wants love, transformation, healing. You can tell it, **"Thank you for showing yourself."**

Is this "mine" or am I picking this up from someone else? Sometimes stuff comes up that is "ours" and sometimes, we are picking up on the energy of the people around us. Maybe we inherited this feeling from family members. For example, there have been times when I've felt anxious for absolutely no reason. My mind comes up with a story to explain the anxiety but I sense that it is not proportional to the situation. I may be picking up on the anxiety of others, taking it on as my own (old habit as an empath) and then trying to deal with it. A simple way to determine this is to ask, **"Is this mine or someone else's?"** **"If this is someone else's, I send this back to whomever it belongs for the good of all."**

If this can't be determined or you feel it is yours, continue the process.

Journal here any thoughts, feelings, images that come up for you

3) I'm so sorry you are feeling_____. Sometimes, saying this to the part of yourself that needs attention is all that is necessary for a shift, but many times, this part wants to tell you the whole story about why and how it feels so badly. **Write down this story even if it doesn't make immediate sense to you**. Don't sugar coat it or be nice about it. Be honest about what you are feeling and your "story" about it.

This is where journaling, art, dance, movement, vocalization can really be helpful. I enjoy journaling so that works well for me. Other times, movement, dance or vocalization have helped.

4) What do you want? (Hint: this is the Divine intention to bring in what you need to feel balanced and aligned to move forward) Once you write until you can't write anymore (or dance, sing, move etc.), the question, **"What do you want?"** may come up. Good question! **Visualize your "part" asking this question- "what do I want?" Allow yourself to be curious and write down any images or words that come up. Whenever a request is made from this separated part that answers "What do you want?", visualize you giving it to yourself. Reach out with your hands and pull it into your heart.** It may take several tries since this part may have never been asked this or was never heard when she told you what she needed and wanted.

5) **I love you.** I realized so many times during the journaling that **I was loving this part.** Sometimes being present with her was enough for her to know I loved her. Sometimes I had to say, "I love you" or visualize hugging her, holding her on my lap etc. **Here's a great opportunity for writing down how much you love this part.**

6) **"Thank you for keeping me safe."** We said *thank you*, in the beginning, to acknowledge the presence- thanks for showing yourself. Now we are **thanking this part for being there all those years; years of protection, guidance, sacrifice, suffering.** As you love this part, it **no longer has to suffer and do things in the old way**. It has your **attention, love, compassion, understanding**. It is starting to trust that you will respond. It is starting to trust that it can be part of the Whole (which it already is but hasn't been feeling it). Give thanks for all of this resolving **perfectly**. This **sets the intention** for the perfect resolution to happen. **Make it official** by writing it down, dancing it out, vocalizing it!

Creating positive change with the 6 game-changer steps

Once you've read through these 6 steps, do them in order. Write down anything you need to, read it out loud, imagine yourself comforting your part as they tell their tale, ask for what they need, and give it to them. Writing, reading out loud and visualizing it all resolving itself repaves your brain (it helps your brain rehearse what you want) so you can move forward and do what you need to do. There will be times when you have the opportunity, time, space to use all these steps. In the beginning, it will feel like you are taking a lot of time going through everything. It may take time to stop, listen, write, and process. However, what I have found is that as you get practiced with this process, it doesn't have to take but a few moments.

Often, if you acknowledge that you are having a feeling, things shift. Other times, you are in such overwhelm that it isn't until later that you realize that self-compassion was needed. Do the steps as soon as you are able. Ultimately, it really doesn't matter because you will learn and expand along the way at your own pace.

I've found that there are times when something comes up and immediately I know what to do. I excuse myself to do the steps. "Gotta go to the ladies' room!" (no one can argue with that). And then come back with a new view. Doing that actually has led to me looking forward to situations where I feel that trigger (seriously!) because I know it means that I'm going to find out more about myself. It reveals what beliefs I hold, and that I will be rewarded for this step outside my comfort zone.

Example:
"Good Girl" battles "Mean Girl" – in my head

Not too long ago, I discovered a part of me that had had ENOUGH. She had enough of people crossing her boundaries, dominating the space and making themselves the focus of attention. What once was tolerated, rationalized, glossed over could no longer be ignored. It was almost frightening to other parts of me how strongly this part was screaming about how fed up she was. I felt this part getting really snide (I'm not even going to tell you what was said...) and mean about another person- she had had it! She wanted to lash out. My 'Good Girl' part (who didn't rock the boat, was passive, and nice) was freaked out because my "Mean Girl" part entered the scene.

So, I started journaling in a "Mean Girl" journal (I felt naughty and liberated!). I realized that this "Mean Girl" part was important. She was watching out for me, she was telling me to protect my boundaries and stand my ground. She wanted to act out, but I knew that before anything was to happen, I needed to express all this on paper and get it out. I journaled and journaled and cried and read what I had written. I wrote until I ran out of things to say.

I asked the "Mean Girl", "What do you want?" (Step 4). Good question. This "Mean Girl" wanted to be able to express herself clearly, regardless of the consequences. This was a big challenge for me. My "Good Girl" was then activated – what if this person hates me? What if I ruin the relationship? I had to give that part self-compassion, understanding, gratitude, and hear her story. Wow! This mini soap opera ("The Bold and the *Ritaful*"?) taught me so much about how I was operating in conflict. I was not in my full power

What about the desire to alleviate the distress? Of course, when you feel compassion you don't want others to suffer. However, you do see the necessity of going through something uncomfortable or even tragic as a possible vehicle for growth. You don't wish anything painful on anyone and yet at the same time, you can see the opportunity to use pain as a catalyst for change, expansion, deeper understanding, and more compassion. From my perch, often the alleviation of the distress starts with being a compassionate ally to those who suffer. Sometimes that requires action but many times, it's about holding space for a friend, neighbor, loved one or stranger. Anything that comes after compassion is always for the highest good. Why? Because anything that comes when you are in a higher state of consciousness has the power of that higher state behind it. When you are allowing the Divine to flow through you, you are allowing the Divine to work through you.

because these two parts (along with some other parts) were working against each other trying to help me. I asked my "Good Girl" what she wanted- which was to do this as kindly as possible and to love myself no matter what.

I ended up communicating my needs clearly and kindly (it *can* be done). Things unfolded in amazing ways. The energy shifted and I realized that hanging out with people who have a hard time with boundaries taught me how important my boundaries are for my well-being. I also learned that all of my parts are there to protect me- and were much more effective when I listen to them with compassion and allow them to work with the whole. I realized that it was time to let some relationships go. I understood that this doesn't mean I'm a bad person and allowed that to happen.

Another example: "Bad Mom"

Here's a story of someone using the six steps of the Game Changer and dove into self-compassion:

"When my kids were infants and toddlers, it was kinda crazy around here. Every morning, we'd be climbing into the van, buckling in, and going to pre-school. We were always very late and rushed. One particularly chaotic morning, I lost my cool. My toddler would not get into her seat and we were going to be very late...again. Against all judgement, I shoved her into her booster pushed her hips into the seat and buckled her up with the rage of a mad woman. It was ugly. She was fighting me and I didn't care. I wanted car seat revenge. I wanted control....even as my behavior was very much out of control. After I realized what I just did, I started to cry. Who had I become? I was an angry, unreasonable person dealing with a little toddler, but what's worse, I really didn't care that she was being angry and unreasonable. I got my car seat revenge, but at what cost?

I had to do some real soul searching (aka Game Changer writing) to hear out that part who had that story.

When I had a quiet moment, I just let myself feel what I was feeling (Step 1). Anger, frustration, guilt, rage, and remorse all came up. I felt tension and tightness in my chest and jaw. I put my hands over my heart and sent it love. I closed my eyes and visualized light going to my heart. Although it felt weird, I thanked the emotions for coming up and showing themselves (Step 2). I realized that it was giving me a clue about what was really going on inside me. I felt the feelings were mine, but just in case, I told them to go back to whomever they belonged for the good of all. Then, I dove into Step 3 and said "I'm sorry you are feeling this frustration, anger, rage, guilt, and remorse" over and over again. I journaled what came up. It was a scene of being trapped in this world of motherhood where I was 'damned if I do, damned if I don't'. Where the standards felt impossible to meet. I had to be 'perfect'; have 'perfect' kids, and get to places on time without difficulty. I imagined teachers making judgments about me and my kids because we were late so often. This part of me felt defeated and exhausted because she had all the responsibility and no authority. This part felt like a 'bad mom'. When I asked what she wanted (Step 4), she said 'A break. I want to not be judged. I want to not be rushing if we're late. I want my kids to listen to me.' I realized that I had no control over being late or what the teachers thought of us, but I could refrain from judging this part. I could give her the authority to be late if she needed without the internal condemnation (yet another part who I named 'Judgy Mom' also needed to have a dialogue). I realized that this part had created a fictitious internal "Mom Manual" which held these unattainable standards. Most importantly, by becoming aware all of this mental drama I had created, I realized that could put and end to the drama (anger, shame, blame, sadness) and I could rewrite that manual -or just throw it out!

I told this part that I would not judge when things didn't go as planned. I was going to give myself a break. I was also going to slow down, regardless of how late we were, so I didn't rush anyone. I told this part that I love her (Step 5) and in my imagination, we had a good hug. Lastly, I thanked her for keeping me safe and trying so hard to keep things going (Step 6). I told her that I would keep connected and in communication whenever things were getting crazy so we could work together without judgment. I wrote that intention and pledge out in my journal.

Not surprisingly, once I did this process and made the commitment without the judgement, we slowed down the process, things went smoother and we were on time much more than before. And when we were late, it was OK. I accepted that sometimes we were going to be late. It took some time, but it was worth it to connect with this part of me who felt so 'not enough' as a mother and a person. Not only did it change the dynamic with my kids, it changed how they saw me. Calmer, more mindful, more loving, and with more authority." —J.D.

Your journal space (just in case you need it!)

"Acceptance doesn't mean resignation: it means understanding something is what it is and that there's got to be a way through it" —Michael J. Fox

ACCEPTANCE

Part 2

"Acceptance is when you abide with the Divine."
—Rita Desnoyers-Garcia

The next important step in your pursuit of self-compassion is *acceptance*. It is key to integrating your Soul and fully loving yourself.

Acceptance is seeing things the way they are and not the way we need or want to see them. It is being in the NOW about life. It is about fully being present. It is about being non-resistant to yourself or your situations. It is about recognizing that everything is changing all the time. There is no permanence in the physical world.

Acceptance is NOT resignation nor giving up. It is not about being passive, though it is not always active. This is not to say you can't change your situation, and in fact, acceptance allows for the most elegant changes to unfold in Divine time. This is not some spiritual mumbo-jumbo where I list opposites to impress you. It's how it works...keep reading!

The first step is acknowledging what feels unacceptable. You must accept where you are. If you don't, you'll never really move forward. You'll stay stuck if you can't abide with where you are right now in this moment. You are exactly where you are supposed to be. (I'm not B.S.-ing you.) You're not behind- you're not going too slow. You're not going backward. You are perfectly situated. *All the time.* Once you understand that, *everything* becomes much easier. It's amazing. It's not that everything magically changes but your perception of reality changes. There's psychological space where before you may have felt no space. As you accept where you are in the process of becoming, you can then accept your life situation.

At this point, people like to bring up dramatic situations. How can you accept the death of a loved one? A fatal diagnosis? War or starvation or torture?

That is your mind trying to come up with reasons to not accept. Push pause on the instinct to resist and ask this question instead: Can I accept where I am in this process? The weather outside? That I forgot to buy coffee? Can I accept that I feel tired or angry or jealous or afraid? Can I accept this moment? That I haven't figured this out yet? That I experience this as unacceptable? If I accept this then _____ (i.e. I will be vulnerable to harm, nothing will change.)

Also notice that by not accepting, you've paid dearly for it (amiright?). You've felt lots of strong feelings, and you've denied feelings. You've repressed, betrayed, felt stuck, suffered greatly from non-acceptance. Perhaps non-acceptance has made you sick, caused you to lash out, hurt people, judge yourself and others. You know what happens when you resist life - you've lived that over and over.

Are you the least bit curious about what would happen if you allowed yourself to accept this moment? **Did anything come up when you asked these questions?** Take advantage of the space below to **write/draw about it**.

Feeling into the now

Close your eyes. Take three slow breaths and allow yourself to come to center. Now, feel into this moment. You may have a lot of thoughts that swirl around. Let them come and go. Now...can you accept this moment?

With any sensations, thoughts, feelings, swirling around- come into this space. Can you accept all of this as an experience happening?

How was that? What did you notice? How did you feel? Record any thoughts or feelings.

Exercise
1

This is something that you can do each moment of each day. In the beginning, try this when you're in line or at a traffic light or washing your hands. I know I called this a "project" but it's really **a practice**. Yes, I fooled you. Sorry. It was for your own good. You can feel what you are feeling- witnessing it instead of getting caught up in it and going down the usual road.

When you bring together acceptance of where you are and self-compassion, a kind of alchemy happens. It transforms *you* and then the situation. You feel or perceive things differently within you, and later perhaps the outside situation shifts. There's space. There are other options not previously seen.

Why? Because you allowed your Divinity (aka Higher Divine Self) to come through. When you allow innate Divinity to come through you have Divine Power behind you. You are working *with* the Universe. You're not depleting your energy swimming against the current of life. (That's tiring!) You are becoming your own best friend (besties 4 eva!). The ego/personality is becoming practiced in letting Divinity lead and becoming more comfortable and confident with that. The Divine *blends* with you. The Divine is your *best friend*. Rely on Her! High Five!

She is your confidant, your support, your unconditionally loving partner, your nurturer, your teacher. The Divine is not "out there" or separate from you. The Divine *is you*! Not your personality but your essence. When you feel into your essence, you are tapping into Divinity Herself.

Here's another short exercise that you can use over and over throughout the day. See what happens when you do.

Grounding yourself

Sit in a comfortable chair or on the floor or pillow with back straight but relaxed. Close your eyes. Take three deep breaths in through the nose and out through the mouth. Feel yourself come to center. Breathe normally and with each breath, allow yourself to relax a bit. Keep your focus on your breath for a few moments.

Then, as you are ready, see if you can just observe what's going on around you- listening to the wind blowing or the birds singing or cars going by. Whatever is happening, you are quietly observing without comment or labeling or judgment. See if you can hear the silence behind the sounds around you. The stillness that is always there just beyond the movement and sound. See if you can connect with that stillness and silence within you. Practice this for a few minutes. When you are ready, allow yourself to open your eyes and observe your surroundings – once again, without labels or judgment.

Doing this observation meditation just a few minutes a day or throughout your day will help you cultivate patience, stillness, and acceptance of what is.

ACCEPTANCE

Exercise
2

Acceptance + brutal honesty = world peace?

When you allow yourself to accept, you are being self-compassionate. You are accepting where you are, who you are, what's going on, what's not going on. Acceptance allows self-compassion and self-compassion sets the stage for acceptance (cool or what?). Both are a catalyst for Divinity to come through you. Both allow for universal energy to support you, propel you, heal you, connect with you.

It can be really hard sometimes to accept what is. Sometimes it is difficult to accept ourselves, the way we are, or what's going on in the world. At the moment of this writing, there are tragic, horrific events happening in the world. People are being slaughtered, children are starving, people are being poisoned, the Earth is suffering from abuse and is responding with natural explosions, flooding, drought, disease. People are hating on each other. Innocent people are being arrested and executed. Children are being trafficked, abused, killed. People are profiting from all of this one way or another while others are in abject poverty.

How does one accept any of that? It's not about liking it or not wanting it to change or saving anyone or wanting to go after people doing harm. It is about clearly seeing what is...at this moment. It is about seeing yourself clearly...without judgment. You can use your discernment to see what works or what doesn't and be without judgment. Or at least, accept that you are in judgment. We are human, after all.

The trick is to be honest, brutally honest, with yourself. If you are feeling pain, accept that you are experiencing pain. **Don't resist it, just accept it**. Pain is present for right now. You don't have to get lost in it. You don't have to resist it. You don't have to explain it. You can decide to release it right now. And if you can't accept it, you can decide to accept that you can't accept it. You can even laugh at how hard it is to accept. (I've totally done that, so don't knock it until you've tried it.)

Accepting is 80% of letting it go (actually, it's 77% to 83% with a deviation of plus or minus 3%). When you accept what's going on and what you are feeling, you can then allow self-compassion in which will, in turn, increase your acceptance of yourself and affect change. Allowing acceptance and self-compassion often shifts not only your perception and response but the situation itself. Often, nothing more than your own internal acceptance and self-compassion is necessary.

Our acceptance and self-compassion will not stop war or starvation but it will allow us to respond differently to these most difficult of situations. As more and more of us accept and have self-compassion, we join our forces with Universal energy to affect major change with these larger world problems. Through this shift, we come to see the power we possess together, the courage we muster to speak out or take action, and how love reveals truth and moves mountains. Our self-compassion and acceptance becomes compassion for all humankind, the animal world, the plant world, all of the Earth and our Universe.

Action through acceptance

The only way to understand how to act from a place of acceptance is to experience acceptance or allow acceptance to flow through you- even if it's just "I accept that I can't accept this right now" and see what, if any, action is necessary.

Sometimes, with things that feel "unacceptable"- a child's death, any big loss, injustice, you must accept that you can't accept what is happening right now. You can accept that you feel lost, angry, resistant, overwhelmed, or sad. Allow all that to come in and accept it for what it is- deep emotion necessary to cope with something really difficult. Accepting where you are in the "unacceptable" is all you can and need to do.

Example:
"Does anyone else see this?"

One of the themes that comes up over and over again for me is when I find myself asking **"Does anyone else see this?"**. I get a sense that I am alone in my observations and judgments. I am not part of the tribal think. I am seeing something wrong with how the world is working and I seem to be the only one. It's lonely, and many times, it makes me deeply doubt myself or think I may be a bit crazy.

As I started doing the self-compassion and acceptance work, I saw this theme come up again and again in various situations. I wondered more about why this happens and if it's even real or just imagined.

I realized that from a very early age, I had first-hand experiences that were dismissed or labeled "not real," but they felt real to me. I also realized that often I thought or felt differently about something than my family or community felt. I was so young that I didn't have the verbal skills to express this or even fully understand it beyond a "feeling". For example, I'd walk into a room and feel the tension in the air. I'd ask what was going on. The response was that nothing was going on. I started to doubt myself and what I was perceiving. And so, as we often do, I put these experiences into a room and locked them up only to see them leak through the cracks under the door or through the wall in odd ways.

I decided to do my self-compassion work and journaled and sang and cried my way through this experience of not being believed or validated as a young person. I started to believe her. I asked her what she needed. I also accepted that the world is the way it is and that may never change. She wanted me on her side. She wanted to express herself without fear and with support. She wanted to stop doubting herself so much.

As I allowed myself to do that while accepting where I was and that the world may never change, I felt an internal shift. I stopped needing to prove things to people. I stopped having to try to get people to see stuff from my perspective. I not only have more compassion for myself but also with others. I didn't have to be so defensive because I didn't have to defend myself against me. I am literally laughing out loud now because I recognize this part coming up to say, "hello, I'm here!". I also discovered that there were many, many people who saw what I saw or felt what I felt. I was not alone! I had a community who supported me as I started to support and believe in myself.

I accepted that the world may never change and yet it was changing before my eyes.

Another example: Can I accept anger?

"A part of me that I began to love on and accept was my anger. The angry part of me was never acceptable before. I denied her, I stuffed her soooo far down that she would morph into the part that would self destruct and find her power in victimization. But, once I understood that self compassion is NOT conditional, it allows for full acceptance and space for ALL parts, I began to listen to her. After she got her raging energy out, mostly through exercise, I listened without interjecting or judgement. It was hard at first to not reframe or shame her for having "unattractive" thoughts or feelings. The more I gave her the space, the more she transformed into this confident, well spoken, diplomatic leader. She was overstuffed and unrefined at first but then once I loved and showed compassion, I was able to take her points into consideration and act from a place of consciousness, not emotion. This whole concept of shifting from conditional to unconditional acceptance of self allowed for many shifts in my personal and professional life." —N.F.

Here's more space in case you're inspired!

"Integration happens when all parts of your being are in harmony."
—Amy Leigh Mercree, *Joyful Living:*
101 Ways to Transform Your Spirit and Revitalize Your Life

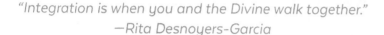

INTEGRATION

Part
3

"Integration is when you and the Divine walk together."
—Rita Desnoyers-Garcia

Integration is about experiencing your wholeness. It's about experiencing all of you. The "good" parts, the "bad" parts, the "happy" parts, the "sad" parts, the "acceptable" and "unacceptable" parts. All of it. All of you gets to be here and is welcomed here. It's my favorite club!

In integration, you bring together all the "parts" that feel they haven't been welcomed in your life by saying "You belong here. You are me. We are coming together, so we stop being against each other. I'm not completely me without you."

It's about allowing any separateness to dissolve - all parts that feel separate can come home. **We are whole always but we may not experience ourselves in that state**. As a result, we have our parts which feel separate, afraid, marginalized, ignored, ungrounded, misunderstood, or unloved. The parts will "act out" to get our attention and love but so many times what they get is dismissed and blamed by other parts. When we have self-compassion and by allowing the Divine that is US to shine through, we are setting ourselves up for integrating these lost 'parts' of our psyche.

Integrating for harmony

When we integrate our parts, we are working **with** them. They are able to serve us instead of us trying to hide, dismiss, repress or cover them. When we integrate our "parts" we work in harmony, in alignment, and with the power of the Universe. The orchestra of our parts play beautiful music together when we are integrated. When we are not, our separate parts are playing out of sync, clashing and drowning each other out in a chaotic mess of sound (chaotic concerts - the worst! Earplugs please!).

One must have self-compassion and acceptance in order to integrate. The experience of "separateness" dissolves in self-compassion and acceptance.

An example: Hiding from money

Like 99.9% of people, I had a real hang up around money. I didn't want to deal with it or take account of it. I had a hard time spending it and felt guilty saving it or even having it. As with many wounds, I was "damned if I do, damned if I don't" around money.

I told my coach about how I didn't even look at our family finances. My husband took on that role and I was happier for it. However, I also felt guilt and shame because I felt like a woman who submitted to her husband when it came to money. My husband never even hinted at the idea that I couldn't or shouldn't deal with our money, but I felt it nevertheless. So "old Rita"...

My coach challenged me on this and asked me to go in and really take a good look at where we were spending, saving, what investments we had and what debts we were paying. I could feel the anxiety and overwhelm begin just thinking about it.

First, I decided to have some self-compassion around this. Yes, I was having difficulties but could I give myself a break? Could I sit with myself and just ask about what's going on and how I was feeling? Could I, as Buddha teaches, "sit and have tea" with these parts of my psyche that panic around money? I learned so much about myself by asking questions, writing my story and asking what I wanted.

I started to accept, in this self-compassion process, that not only did I have some very strong feelings about money, but they started when I was pretty young. My 10-year-old self was totally overwhelmed by all the numbers and feeling responsible for all of this.

Facing my fears and becoming whole

I realized that when I was looking at the accounting, I wasn't looking at it as an adult, but as a 10-year-old child: Someone too young to make sense out of it, much less feel responsible for keeping it all organized and safe.

Then, I talked to this scared, 10-year-old self. I told her that I, as the adult, would not leave her alone with all this and blame her for anything that went "wrong." I was going to take control and relieve her of any responsibility. I was going to learn and then teach her about money. Go, Rita!

I opened up the Quicken page and took my time and really looked at it all. When I didn't understand something and felt the overwhelm, I knew it was my young self and would talk her through it. Breathing, soothing, taking a break and coming back. We got through it. And it wasn't so bad. Nothing terrible happened. In fact, I started to get curious.

Little by little, this 10-year-old part started to trust me and ask questions

with no shame or sense that she needed to carry the burden of making sure our money was in good order. As this occurred, she started to let go of what was so distressing and integrated with me. Instead of a separate part of the psyche trying to get my attention through strong negative emotions, I now had an ally willing to speak up, ask good questions, and trust that if we didn't know something, we could find help and support, learn, and expand. The shame was gone, the guilt was dissolving, and I was acting from a more integrated place.

Another example:
Integration brings and is supported through action

This person experienced Integration in her comedy writing!

"I was 6 weeks away from my stand-up comedy performance and I was stuck. I had done stand-up before; I knew how to write and perform but I was drawing a complete blank this time. I had no quirky observations to share. No snarky commentary. Nothing. There wasn't a funny thought around me for miles. I began to panic. The weeks slowly ticked by and I was still staring at a blank page. What if I couldn't do it? What if I had no material to deliver? People were counting on me for a good laugh (or so I told myself) and I may fail in front of all of them. My anxiety level was sky-high and I was white-knuckling it through the day with thoughts of complete public failure: an unfunny comic. What a shame.

But then I asked the question that turned it all around: Can you have compassion for yourself? Can you have compassion for that part of yourself that is scared and anxious, as well as for the part that is feeling the pressure of being funny on demand? Once I allowed myself to truly see those parts and have compassion for them, it all came together. I recognized these parts of me from my past - childhood parts that were forced to go back to school after a family trauma. Being forced to write a comedy set felt just like being forced to go back to school. . That child wanted to be heard and loved, so I had an imaginary conversation with her. Once she was safely integrated, I wrote all my material in a fast 45 minutes and had a terrific show. Without accepting those parts of me, I'd probably still be looking at a blank page. Giving myself a break turned it all around." —A.M.

Reuniting parts of you

Here are some effective questions to ask yourself and journal about in order to integrate the parts that feel separate. These questions focus on anger and sadness but you can ask them about any emotion you are experiencing:

Exercise 1

Which part of you becomes activated when you feel angry or sad?

....

....

Can you have compassion for that part?

....

....

What does this part have to say to you?

....

....

Now can you feel compassion, love, for that part?

....

....

What do you want to say?

....

....

Can you accept where you are in this situation?

....

....

Can you accept and honor this part?

....

....

What does she want? Remember that asking, honoring and giving your separate parts what they need/want helps them to trust, let go of the burden, and integrate into the whole.

....

....

Can you give her what she wants? Be honest here. Even if you don't know how to give her what she wants, listen to the request and let her know you will do your best to attend to her needs. It may take some "sit-downs" to hear what she really needs and to give it to her.

Now that you've gone through the process, what did you notice? What did you feel? What did you witness? Journal it now.

How do you feel now? Better/worse/the same?

Can you see how this part helped you in life? Can you see how she's gotten you here? Do you see the limits of her reaction/responses? How can you help her?

Can you see how the anger went from "dangerous" to "powerful"? Did it change at all?

Can you see that this part can be an integral part of you as she feels your love and acceptance?

How could you wield her power the next time you experience anger or sadness?

....

....

....

....

How would you interact with her the next time she pops up in your awareness?

....

....

....

....

Can you ask her if she feels honored and recognized enough to work with you in an integrated way?

....

....

....

....

Does she want to sit at your table with you?

....

....

....

....

Some words about gratitude

While the phrase "an attitude of gratitude" has been overused, I want to emphasize that being in a state of gratitude and appreciation is crucial in all stages of your work of Self-compassion, Acceptance, and Integration. Be grateful for yourself, where you are, and where you want to be. Gratitude keeps your focus on where you are going, creates more for which to be grateful, and it keeps you energetically positive. Gratitude fuels you (complaining drains you). Gratitude keeps you motivated by love and not fear. It works so well that I conjure gratitude daily, if not moment to moment - through writing, speaking, visualizing, and doing. It's not just a self-motivational mantra, it is an energetic law.

How long does integration take?

Sometimes, this process takes no time at all but many times, it can take minutes, hours, days, weeks, years. It all depends on you and what you are trying to have self-compassion for, accept, and integrate. Some parts of us are so ready to reunite that it almost feels instantaneous and the next logical step. Either way, it's worth it, don't you think? (Answer: It's worth it!) And you'll never be done. There's always more to feel, experience, learn from, grow from, and integrate. That's why we're here after all.

If you're having a tough time integrating, know this

When you are allowing for self-compassion and acceptance, you are claiming the seat of the Divine Heart within you. From that new perch, you start to loosen up any bit that needs compassion or acceptance or to be seen, heard, or recognized. You are kicking up dust that has laid dormant for a long time, in some cases. As you integrate these bits of dust (coughcough!) and parts of the psyche, you experience them again as things are released, reclaimed, reoriented.

Think of it as a house renovation. You have to demolish the old before you build the new. Dust and pieces of wood, metal, cabinets, ceiling fans are all taken down. Some are thrown out, cleaned up, refurbished, moved, reinstalled. It's a mess at first (then the contractor disappears for 3 weeks!). It may feel really overwhelming if you don't have a plan or know that you are rebuilding and not just losing the walls! With each part being disassembled, you get to examine it and decide- does this stay for the new space or go out? It may take some time and you may live somewhere else or in a tiny space for a while as the renovation happens ("Let's microwave mac 'n cheese in the living room!"). However, as time goes on and the work continues, you see things taking shape. As you move forward and stay focused, you are amazed by what is created.

GOING FORWARD

You did it!

Congratulations on getting to the end of this book.

Phew!

Maybe you just read it through and haven't really done any exercises yet. I encourage you to go back and really allow yourself the time to do the self-compassion steps and stay with the difficult feelings enough to write down who is feeling them and what they are saying about them. Allow yourself time to write it all out. Then ask the important question "What do you want and need right now?" This calls forth your intention of actually giving yourself what you need to walk down a new road instead of staying stuck on the old one. Reread the **Acceptance** and **Integration** chapters and go through the exercises. In the beginning, these things take a bit of time but soon they will become how you do things. This process requires accepting what you are feeling and the situation you find yourself in. Then you can integrate the new ways and address your inner needs so you can become whole and walk the new integrated, compassionate path.

Like any self-help book, value only comes in **taking it off the shelf or your nightstand and reading it and doing the work. (That's a hint.)**

Here's how to get maximum value from this book:

Use as many opportunities to do the work as possible

If you feel something negative within yourself, start allowing yourself to feel it instead of repressing, stifling, or avoiding. Sometimes you don't have to journal what you are feeling, you just need to allow yourself to release and soothe. Thank yourself and listen to what you need. Ask the necessary questions and most often, even as you integrate, notice familiar stuff come up so you know what you need. This process has brought me a wealth of other tools that I borrow from other teachers and organizations. As I have become more self-compassionate, I've found others on the compassion path who are interested, open, and eager to feel better about themselves and others and how to respond to the lack of compassion in our world.

One of the best ways for me to keep on this path is joining with others (I get to tell them jokes!). I have taught *The Compassion Course* (from which this book has come) and that has kept me in my heart, full of compassion, and true to my word. As students graduated, we formed *Compassion Circles* where we discuss how we **incorporate these practices in our everyday lives**. It's **Self-Compassion, Acceptance, Integration in action**. Once again, it reinforces the process, supports us, rejuvenates us, and allows us to bring our compassion into the world.

EXERCISES + STRATEGIES

At a glance

Self-Compassion Strategy #1: Calm The Storm

The mechanics of self-compassion are pretty simple.   Start with the breath.

Going inward for a moment, taking a breath and letting it out, can be an act of self-compassion. It may not stop your mind from badgering you, but it will start a process to relax a bit and release some tension. Compassion is about relaxing internally. When we breathe through the nose deeply and exhale gently through the mouth, we signal to the body to relax, slow down. When the body can relax a bit, we are better able to observe our minds going all over the place in thought. When we can observe ourselves, we take on the perspective of the compassionate self. We separate a bit from the idea that we are our thoughts or trapped in our situation. When we relax in our bodies through our breath, we are more likely to feel some compassion come through. Focused, relaxed breathing calms the storm of thoughts and emotions inside.

So take a moment to come to center. Sometimes, doing that is enough. Take a moment to breathe in and out through the nose and out the mouth. Jot down how you feel afterward. You can use this whenever you need it during the day.

Self-Compassion Strategy #2: Switch It

When breathing is not doing it for you, there are other things to do! Here's a process I use when I have a negative feeling:

Allow yourself to feel what you feel- name it, identify it; sadness, boredom, anger, etc. Then see the opposite of that; joy, excitement, calm, etc. Say to yourself, "May I bring more joy/excitement/calm into my life". You are calling in what you need to come back to balance. You don't feel any lack. You are calling your desired state forth from the Divine within. This is what self-compassion and acceptance does; it puts you in a state of the Divine so you can have room for something new.

Sometimes it takes more effort because you're really "in it." You're in your head. The story of how you messed up or how things are not working out the way you planned or "you have really done it now!" That anxious, tormented thinking leads to behaviors to "fix" things, act out, numb etc. And here we go!

Self-Compassion Strategy #3: The Game Changer

The following steps are here when you need a little extra help or you are new to this kind of process.

1) **Feel what you are feeling.** You are feeling something as a result of perceiving your world. Your perceptions are based on your personal, familial, and societal history. We decide something feels "good" or "bad", "beautiful," "ugly," etc. We have thoughts- and we have feelings about those thoughts. One of the first things we tend to do when we feel anything (especially a negative feeling), is ignore, avoid, or rationalize. When was the last time you felt what you felt? Take a moment to feel into what's happening within you right now. Maybe it feels frightening to really feel the anxiety or hatred or jealousy. Recognize and acknowledge that you are having a feeling experience. You may blame this feeling on the actions of another (and that may be very valid), but many times that deflects from feeling the emotion.

Take a moment, close your eyes and feel what you feel. Connect to your body. Are their areas in your body where you feel tension, constriction, or pain? Put your hand there, breathe into that area, and send it love and compassion.

2) Thank this part for showing itself! Sometimes your feeling is an expression of a "part" of you that needs attention and is telling you something. Perhaps it has been there for years, to warn you and protect you. Maybe it got you through your childhood and was a survival mechanism. You may have been discouraged from listening to it. It's up for a reason; to be expressed, heard, and to serve you. It also wants love, transformation, healing. You can tell it, "Thank you for showing yourself."

Is this "mine" or am I picking this up from someone else? Sometimes stuff comes up that is "ours" and sometimes, we are picking up on the energy of the people around us. Maybe we inherited this feeling from family members. For example, there have been times when I've felt anxious for absolutely no reason. My mind comes up with a story to explain the anxiety but I sense that it is not proportional to the situation. I may be picking up on the anxiety of others, taking it on as my own (old habit as an empath) and then trying to deal with it. A simple way to determine this is to ask, "Is this mine or someone else's?" "If this is someone else's, I send this back to whomever it belongs for the good of all." If this can't be determined or you feel it is yours, continue the process.

3) I'm so sorry you are feeling _____ . Sometimes, saying this to the part of yourself that needs attention is all that is necessary for a shift, but many times, this part wants to tell you the whole story about why and how it feels so badly. Write down this story even if it doesn't make immediate sense to you. Don't sugar coat it or be nice about it. Be honest about what you are feeling and your "story" about it. This is where journaling, art, dance, movement, vocalization can really be helpful. I enjoy journaling so that works well for me. Other times, movement, dance or vocalization have helped.

4) What do you want? (Hint: *this is the Divine intention to bring in what you need to feel balanced and aligned to move forward*) Once you write until you can't write anymore (or dance, sing, move, etc.), the question, "What do you want?" may come up. Good question! Visualize your part asking this question- what does she/he want? Allow yourself to be curious and write down any images or words that come up. Whenever a request is made from this separated part that answers "What do you

want?", visualize giving it to yourself. Reach out with your hands and pull it into your heart. It may take several tries since this part may have never been asked this or was never heard when she told you what she needed and wanted.

5) I love you. I realized so many times during the journaling that I was loving this part. Sometimes being present with her was enough for her to know I loved her. Sometimes I had to say, "I love you" or visualize hugging her, holding her on my lap, etc.

6) "Thank you for keeping me safe." We said *thank you*, in the beginning, to acknowledge the presence- thanks for showing yourself. Now we are thanking this part for being there all those years; years of protection, guidance, sacrifice, suffering. As you love this part, it no longer has to suffer and do things in the old way. It has your attention, love, compassion, understanding. It is starting to trust that you will respond. It is starting to trust that it can be part of the Whole (which it already is, but hasn't been feeling it). Give thanks for all of this resolving perfectly. This sets the intention for the perfect resolution to happen.

Acceptance Exercise #1: Feeling Into The Now

Close your eyes. Take three slow breaths and allow yourself to come to center. Now, feel into this moment. You may have a lot of thoughts that swirl around. Let them come and go. Now...can you accept this moment?

With any sensations, thoughts, feelings, swirling around- come into this space. Can you accept all of this as an experience happening?

How was that? What did you notice? How did you feel?

Acceptance Exercise #2: Grounding Yourself

Sit in a comfortable chair or on the floor or pillow with back straight but relaxed. Close your eyes. Take three deep breaths in through the nose and out through the mouth. Feel yourself come to center. Breathe normally and with each breath, allow yourself to relax a bit. Keep your focus on your breath for a few moments.

Then, as you are ready, see if you can observe what's going on around you- listening to the wind blowing or the birds singing or cars going by. Whatever is happening, you are quietly observing without comment or labeling or judgment. See if you can hear the silence behind the sounds around you. The stillness that is always there beyond the movement and sound. See if you can connect with that stillness and silence within you. Practice this for a few minutes. When you are ready, allow yourself to open your eyes and observe your surroundings – once again without labels or judgment.

Doing this observation meditation a few minutes a day or throughout your day will help you cultivate patience, stillness, and acceptance of what is.

Integration Exercise: Reuniting Parts Of You

Here are some effective questions to ask yourself and journal about in order to integrate the parts that feel separate. These questions focus on anger and sadness but you can ask them about any emotion you are experiencing:

Which part of you becomes activated when you feel angry or sad?

Can you have compassion for that part?

What does this part have to say to you?

Now can you feel love for that part?

What do you want to say?

Can you accept where you are in this situation?

Can you accept and honor this part?

What does she want? Remember that asking, honoring and giving your separate parts what they need/want helps them to trust, let go of the burden, and integrate into the whole.

Can you give her what she wants? Be honest here. Even if you don't know how to give her what she wants, listen to the request and let her/him know you will do your best to attend to her needs. It may take some "sit-downs" to hear what she really needs and to give it to her.

Now that you've gone through the process, what did you notice? What did you feel? What did you witness? Journal it now.

How do you feel now? Better/worse/the same?

Can you see how this part helped you in life? Can you see how she's gotten you here? Do you see the limits of her reaction/responses? How can you help her?

Can you see how the anger went from "dangerous" to "powerful"? Did it change at all?

Can you see that this part can be an integral part of you as she feels your love and acceptance?

How could you wield her power the next time you experience anger or sadness?

How would you interact with her the next time she pops up in your awareness?

Can you ask her if she feels honored and recognized enough to work with you in an integrated way?

Does she want to sit at your table with you?

45

ACKNOWLEDGEMENTS

Thank you!

It is always a challenge to thank everyone who supported me throughout my journey so that I could write this book. Personal friends, family, strangers, teachers, mentors, and coaches were all part of it. However, some people stand out in particular. Kathy Kirk and Diana Luna who are friends, participants, supporters, mentors, and ambassadors of my work. If they weren't game for this, it may never have happened. Amy McGlinn who took my first draft and helped me create something that would attract, speak to, and encourage people to actually use for their benefit and walked with me all the way to the end. To my friend and layout designer Stacey Houghtaling who made this project more understandable, attractive, and accessible through her superpowers of color, font, art, and design and for Heather Kern, who designed the final interior and cover. For all my Beta-Readers who were brave and generous enough to see if what I wrote would work for them. I am humbled and grateful for your feedback and willingness! My former coach Chris Sarris, who worked with me probably at my most vulnerable for four years. You have taught me so much and supported me as I started to teach and coach others. To all my clients and friends who were trusting enough to allow me into their lives and hearts, to see the vulnerable places and be open enough to listen and take in my two cents and support. You are beyond courageous! My husband Enrique who always supports my growth and expansion. If that's not love, I don't know what is! To my kids, who I try to impart my wisdom and more often than not, I learn so much and find that I am the student...I am humbled and honored to be your mother.

CPSIA information can be obtained
at www.ICGtesting.com
Printed in the USA
BVHW060835050619

550185BV00001B/1/P